BOA
EDITIONS
LIMITED

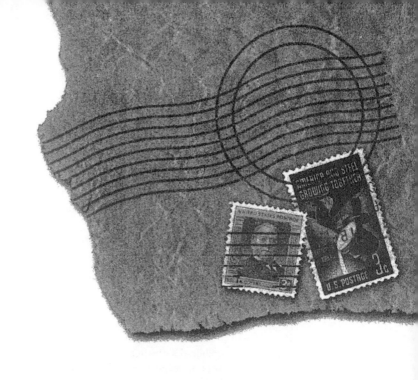

PLUS SHIPPING

Poems by
Bob Hicok

BOA EDITIONS, LTD. — ROCHESTER, NEW YORK — 1998

LC #: 98–72193
ISBN: 1–880238–67–5

First Edition
98 99 00 01 7 6 5 4 3 2

Publications by BOA Editions, Ltd.—
a not-for-profit corporation under section 501 (c) (3)
of the United States Internal Revenue Code—
are made possible with the assistance of grants from
the Literature Program of the New York State Council on the Arts,
the Literature Program of the National Endowment for the Arts,
the Lannan Foundation, the Sonia Raiziss Giop Charitable Foundation,
as well as from the Mary S. Mulligan Charitable Trust,
the County of Monroe, NY,
and from many individual supporters.

Cover Design: Nancy David
Cover Art: Center panel from "Pan American Unity" by Diego Rivera,
Courtesy of City College of San Francisco
Typesetting: Richard Foerster
Manufacturing: McNaughton & Gunn
BOA Logo: Mirko

BOA Editions, Ltd.
Richard Garth, Chair
A. Poulin, Jr., President & Founder (1976–1996)
260 East Avenue
Rochester, NY 14604

for Eve

Did I shave my legs for this?
—Deana Carter

CONTENTS

ONCE

HEROIN

Imagine spring's thaw, your brother said,
each house a small rain, the eaves muttering
like rivers and you the white skin
the world sheds, your flesh unfolded

and absorbed. You walked Newark together,
tie loosened, a silk rainbow undone,
his fatigues the flat green of summer's end,
all blood drained from the horizon.

It would have been easier had you music
to discuss, a common love for one
of the brutal sports, if you shared
his faith that breath and sumac are more

alike than distinct, mutations of the same
tenacity. You almost tried it for him,
cinched a belt around your arm, aimed
a needle at the bloated vein, your window

open to July's gaunt wind and the radio
dispersing its chatty somnolence. When
he grabbed your wrist, his rightful face
came back for a moment: he was fifteen

and standing above Albert Ramos, fists
clenched, telling the boy in a voice
from the Old Testament what he'd do if certain
cruelties happened again. Loosening the belt,

you walked out, each straight and shaking,
into the hammering sun, talked of the past
as if it were a painting of a harvested field,
two men leaning against dusk and pitchforks.

That night he curled up and began to die,
his body a pile of ants and you on the floor
ripping magazines into a mound of words
and faces, touching his forehead with the back

of your hand in a ritual of distress, fading
into the crickets' metered hallucination.
When in two days he was human again, when
his eyes registered the scriptures of light,

when he tried to stand but fell and tried
again, you were proud but immediately
began counting days, began thinking
his name were written in a book

locked in the safe of a sunken ship,
a sound belonging to water, to history,
and let him go, relinquished him
to the strenuous work of vanishing.

LOUISE

She said I looked like Jesus and it was true. I looked
    like the Jesus of Dayton
    and Topeka, black hair brushing my shoulders and thin

as martyrdom, flesh denied but not vanquished, eyes blue
    and deep-set, shadowed
    like those in paintings she'd grown up with, the Savior

of dining rooms and VFW halls. A maid forever, she'd lived
    on her knees, black
    skin crosshatched with a web of white lines,

which from a distance looked like powder. We worked in a home
    for the retarded,
    each man having fallen from the womb with key

chromosomes snapped, though where I saw accident she found
    plan. She talked
    to God and God talked back, a running conversation

about degreasers, her son, the cabdriver from Trinidad
    who refused to right
    the cross hanging upside-down from his mirror. Crazy

if you'd just met her, determined if you knew she was eighty,
    alone, poor
    because she believed the nonsense about love

and grace as discovered in acts rather than words, meaning
    canned peaches, Wonder
    Bread, even the transistor that no longer caught

any music that floated above 95 on the AM dial, were given
    to kids and junkies
    without question, without doubt that all human needs

are divine. My last day she asked that I stand in a doorway
        for a picture. And
        I was good, didn't ask if she perceived the irony

of a black believer wanting the image of a white agnostic,
        but smiled, allowed her
        to adjust my hair, and tried my best to suppose

redemption was not only warranted but possible, that
        I could hang
        from a cross and think of anything but revenge.

Plus Shipping

Inspired by Kokopelli, Golfer-Pelli is a fun-loving
symbol for our times.
    —from one of the 400 mail-order catalogs we
    received last year

Certainly it was a premonition of a Navajo warrior that men
in plaid would take up sticks and club a ball into a hole's

submission. And that a god of prosperity and joy, flute
player, source of the wind's conversational obsessions,

secretly longed to represent the beef-fatted, tax-sheltered,
divot-spewing tribe in their hunger for real estate

made green and blemish-free, acres of fertilized eternity.
It happened like this: someone named Stan or Rita

spanked their cell-phone open in Manhattan traffic, called
Lou Ellen or Robbie and went on at an ecstatic pitch

about a program they saw on the Learning Channel last night
that documented cave paintings in Arizona of this guy

with hair like spiders and a body twisted as if
he'd swallowed a hurricane, and wouldn't it make a hot

knickknack if we put him in knickers with a seven iron
in his hands? And later, after the market research,

after paying one company to come up with a name, another
to design the eyes, hips, the casual-yet-indigenous-gestalt

needed to represent a sport built around the prophecy
of leisure, Stan or Rita will confess to something like

inspiration, a little zing, a small frisson disrupting
their preoccupation with fear that screamed low

cost, high profit. And I wouldn't mind if I were ten
or drunk most of the time, if I'd missed

even half the commercials utilizing the dramatic skills
of Super Bowl quarterbacks, the winks of senators

who reached for president but fell one scandal short,
wouldn't care if I could forget Michael Jackson

trying to sell his crotch, Elizabeth Taylor
hustling the diamonds of her scent, if just once

someone would stand before a camera and simply say
I've made this offensive thing but won't leave you alone

until you send me ten bucks. Golfer-Pelli's destined
for mantles, to fill that hole between vase and clock

where space bleeds, needing the bandage of artifact.
And what of the Buddha alarm clock, Shiva spice rack,

the shoe polisher in which red and green fuzzy wheels
pop from Muhammad's ears and spin your leather clean?

Give it time and you'll get your crack at each
and more, for as we eat and sleep there's someone

flipping through a magazine, strolling the open veins
of ruins, touching forgotten texts, sculpted faces

of a people centuries gone, who can't help but think
there's beauty and sorrow and money in every one of these.

WATCHING WELLES

What he knows: hustling wine to the middle class,
repeating the story of Kane to bankers
who'll trade summaries of his girth and bitterness
for a better place at dinner parties and still

say no. *The most expensive pallet.* To the space
just left of the camera he admits he's wasted
his life. What if this were still New York,
still Macbeth and Mercury and Welles entering a room

like crystal meth does a vein, almost a physical
hallelujah, his haste and power making the weak
mumble *sir*, the strong find suppler ways
of saying yes before they're beaten by the blitz

of his ideas. He was cruel to Marion Davies
as he was brutal to himself: killing Kane on-screen
was suicide, sealed his future as the dead genius,
animate ghost about whom people would say *Didn't he*

make that movie about a sled, wasn't he crushed
by his own weight? Tonight in this small room,
in a small city of a vast country that recycles
every idea, that turns wine into water and legend

into exile, I again hear the newsreel
clack to a stop as shanks of light, a Nazi
trick, make what's not there pivotal, a living
absence. Then a shadow asks after a shadow,

then every form of love is squandered, then a man
attacks a room with the same temper, the exact
flare of Welles going after Houseman with lit
sterno. Cut to the interview,

the twice-dead genius staring to the left
of the camera, to a space where something small
might be, a table with an ashtray, a chair
holding a cup of coffee, when he confides

intimately, simply, that he should have got out,
gone into politics, written books, returned
to the stage after Kane. But how, he asks,
does the addict abstain? And the sigh like he's just

learning, like the hand of God or Caesar's cloak
appears to him, the young Kane's joyous sneer
decades gone and replaced by the bitterness
of having nothing but last words to say.

SUPERSTITION

A broken yoke's three days' rain. Wisteria on the floor
and the bride
won't show. Missed belt loops initiate dissolution, loss
of fortune,
bundling of pain. A cat in different contexts charms
or curses.
A robin in the nave's a fat-time flare, emblem of health
and profit,
though if one strays to a winze miners thrash out,
apprehending
collapse, the living grave. Meaning clings to breath
and follicle,
even tea leaves educate. The hand's wombed fissures,
our jigsawing
of clouds and stars, hold the cunning day accountable,
suggest when best
to taunt and dance, when duck and tremble, mouths sewn,
heads shawled.
At ten I believed the legless nuns that raised hands
arrowed words
upward, assuring my mumbles would be distantly heard.
So nights
I blessed names, parents and friends, dogs and presidents
in turn, asked
the ceiling's spackled swirls to keep their heretical flesh
intact. This habit
begun, obsession followed: I couldn't sleep if I'd left
the listing undone,
a punk-god, codirector of consequence. Then Joseph
Bonafiglio, seeking
a midwestern ocean, climbed a silo and fell in,
got hashed
by the tempered blades of a fan, leaving his parents
a bodiless grief.
My fault, I thought, and gave up prayer, later God whom I'd
mistrusted anyway—

eavesdropper, snoop, Big Brother with all the keys. Yet
I'll still speak
the names of those I love as if the act protects, mediates
the random parceling
of woe and sludge, keeps them happy, sober, in line for the big
promotion. Thistle root
cures toothaches. Rubbing a hand over the head of a bald man
brings the past back,
the picture Technicolor clear. Prayer, mojo, a chicken
nailed to the wall:
like Jesus, sacrificed by the meek; like us, dead after all.

THE APPLICANT

The past's
his Mustang split, front-end pinched around the century
of an oak, the engine shot
by his ear and out the back window,

nasal
septum eaten by coke, veins in arms, between toes, around
genitals thinned, devoured
by relentless needling, is five years

breathless,
hunched inside his own body, trying to sleep and walk
and work transparently,
the words *sky* and *nipple* and *parole*

a dog's
relentless barking. Today he wore a black tie two fingers
wide, white shirt ironed
religiously, creased to withstand

doubt.
Married now, his wife pregnant, he spoke of a second chance,
spun his ring, snapped
the band of his watch and said

please
slowly, as if grafting the sound to air. I wanted to say
but couldn't that it's
a shame desperation's one way

we mark
maturity, that we can look at a sweating man and think,
finally he's grown up.
Really I wanted to ask if it's

possible,
and if so wise, to measure how near one life comes
to being another,
to wonder at the wheel or in bed

if luck
isn't at the center of everything we've thought about god.
We stood, shook hands.
I promised to be quick with an answer.

ONE THING CERTAIN

—for M.C.

He's read
memory's broken, that we hold color
one place, shape another, still
a third for mood, fourth context,
overlays the mind stacks until he's got
oolong tea cooling in a blue cup
on the counter as she cuts
coupons from the Sunday paper. This
is wealth, the prismatic fracture and join.
This is his body held more tightly
to the earth by the gravity
of her ten thousand faces: the shadows
under her lips, the evolving
strokes of age on her forehead, eyes
shaded by wonder and lust, looking up
last September from a book and through
his body, through the false gesture
of walls, to touch a town
and room and child that didn't exist.
Tests show within seconds
recall's fiction, that we create
more than remember. Spoons move, hair
changes color, words enjoy the lives
of clouds, tear and rebundle,
are born from and disappear
into nothing, suggesting slits, apertures
that devour, liberate our lives. Sometimes
he insists he went for bagels,
"London Calling" on the radio, a day
too warm for December and a guy
in line tattooed with a caduceus,
the winged snakes red, his skin
hissing. Or doughnuts, radio off,
the dash pounded so hard it cracked

or he did, or the sky,
or the ground and he drove hard
toward that freedom.
And when he came home,
what kind of quiet, what species
of noise, the extension cord
yellow or orange
and who cares, her body motionless
or swaying, floating as if
overcoming a tedious grip, the story
different depending on fatigue, vodka,
whether he loathes himself or her
more. But no matter how his mind's
tendriled, always the gasp,
the rush of air from her lungs
as he cut and laid her down, a sigh
he never describes as word
or name or soul burning out
but as taunt, a second to believe
her breath was back, to hope
she couldn't die unblessed
by the testament of his shock.

Over Coffee

What you mean to say about the film is that
it moved you, the woman alone at the end
beside a burning field of cane, her brother
carried off in a covered truck to be tortured/
shot. That you're not sure but think
it wasn't about politics but bedrooms
and kitchens. Hands and eyes. The light of dusk
because it stops us on the stairs and makes us
bless a child earnestly chiding her doll
or cherish a crow lifting from an oak, charcoal
smearing blue, when we feel tender and vast
and brittle because the emotions that are hybrids
of anguish and elation are the mediums for spirit's
binding to flesh. But your husband and friends,
up on genres and the lineage of dictators,
wielding jargon like the clipped
phrases of birds who know what the trills signify,
speak of fades, Marxist insinuations,
the opening scene's allegory of whore as El Salvador,
fought over, pierced, beaten by men. They travel
staunchly in the other direction, away from sentiment,
from the image of the woman on her knees
at the edge of a field turning orange, into history,
they abandon the facts of smoke, the muslin dress
given by her husband, her stare as the truck
zippers-up horizon, gets lost in the distance
with its appetite for souls. By the time
they ask your opinion you don't want to talk,
knowing faith dissipates through words,
sure you'll passionately refer to our indebtedness
to memory, suggest that by imagining
the vanished flower, repeating the name
of the lost cat, we retain our lives, webbed
by what we've touched and needed,
the persistence of love despite death an act
of vengeance, a refusal to diminish, you'll swear

the film was about the failure of every good-bye.
All of this you try not to say but do in a clumsy rush
as if the words are falling down, then a pause,
the surrounding chatter coming in like the slurrings
of waves as you hold your breath on a seawall,
then the shift, their eyes dilating in recognition
of conviction, finally the stammers, the rush to be
the first to address this exhilarating stranger.

THE BOND

He gets
robbed, a knife in his chest and two
doctors holding his arms and two
his legs and one pumping blood from his lung
and a scream as constant as the speed
of light because he's not anesthetized
and why oh why the goddamned cigarettes
at 2 A.M.? He heals quickly
because he stops smoking and converts
to a low-sodium diet and learns to meditate
on a window seat with a view of the bay
until his wrists and lips tingle
with the low-voltage love of inner peace.
Life goes back to bananas and dusting
and wanting to ask strangers the history
of their tattoos and looking
for God among the wounded architecture
of factories. Life returns to dreams
of Dolores Del Rio and trying to hold
someone's eyes on the subway long enough
to feel that a discourse of souls
is still possible. The scar entertains
his fingers, is kissed by the woman he loves
as birds must adore the sky, grows so deep
into memory that his body would be broken
without it. For two years he calls the cop
whose voice soothes like Walter
Cronkite's and says
anything with a rising inflection and the cop
says *nothing* like it's the sound
of every breath he takes and hangs up
very softly to apologize. For two years
he pretends he doesn't flinch
at the brown faces and beautiful names
of boys and men who pass on the street
in reds and greens and blues

that could be the colors of a gang
or just light fulfilling its desire to be
everything at once. Then the cop comes by
and says he thinks they got the guy
and the guy's got a hole and the hole's
the last thing he touched. The cop
stops by and asks if he'll come down
and look at the body and he says *of course.*
And he does go down and look at the body
and it is the guy only he says it's not,
only he says he can't remember
these eyes or hands, only he trembles
at the disclosure of the hole and says
he can't recall anything even though
he's carried this face around and beaten
this body and pissed in this mouth every night
for two years of revenge less tangible than wind.
He gets
out, goes home to his rug and plants
and walls that breathe every hundred
years and a view of the bay where water
migrates with constant adoration. He comes
home and strips and lies on the floor
and touches the scar so long that the sound
of cars and feel of his breath and image
of the man on a silver table fuse like glass
rolling red from a furnace. Then it's dusk
and his lover's touching his body like Braille
and asking how his day went, hands and tongue
weightless as ash., —he hears a voice saying *fine,
okay, good,* feels hands on his shoulders
and a tongue circling his nipples, crossing
back and forth over the scar as if erasing,
licking back and forth as if wounds
are what we most dearly love.

WAITING FOR UPS

Now I live inside the window. Now I think the sky
doesn't have enough sky today and that all
the trees have cancer and are whispering
their little coughs to the earth though I don't
hear them because I'm trying to talk
with three boxes destined for Pittsburgh.
The woman from UPS said they'd be here
sometime between eight and five which is like
predicting that one day you'll feel the need
to purchase either a matching rake
and pitchfork or hollow-point bullets
and nightscope. I'm not good at waiting
which means I'm not good at being alive.
I'm not strong enough to believe there must
eventually be a kiss on my spine at midnight
that lasts 47 years and leads to piles
of scrapbooks in which I've recorded
the dailiness of my bliss. I'm not wise enough
to hear anything the ocean has said to me
after worshiping it for days except *go away.*
Gladly I would were it not for these boxes
and the books in the boxes and the letters
between the pages of the books
written by my father to my mother when neither
was dead and therefore suffering
from irretrievable penmanship.
In Pittsburgh my sister wants to open
the boxes and let the words
on the letters molt in her hands and turn
into the voices of our parents
calling us in from a sky turning dark
as a stone's appetite. It's not enough
to send the letters she wants
the books, to hold Pushkin's and Darwin's
embrace of what my father said from a train
on the other side of the country to my mother

in a blue kitchen as she threw
a towel over her shoulder and let sunlight
graze across the paper. She wants to stand
on her porch overlooking a bridge
where strangers practice their hobby
of diving into what they believe is the river's
silence and touch where he signed
                    Love, always love,
because their breaths are mixed in the slight
eternity of ink. If the carrier
ever arrives in her dirt
uniform and bearing the little
computer that will eat my signature
and feed it to a larger
computer that hopes one day to own
all our names, I'll tell her I've thought
from eight to five about why
everything I've concluded thus far
concerning loss is merely a prelude
to a greater confusion. This won't seem
nearly as strange as my insistence
she let me kiss each box good-bye.

A MONKEY

PROCESS OF ELIMINATION

For 71 days I've tried to write about Eichmann
shitting. At no time did this preoccupation
threaten national defense. This is my first
excretory obsession; I wasn't one of those kids
who fish out their little creation,
their sunken boat, and hold it up for mama
like a cat delivering the trophy of a mouse.
I blame a book. I blame Gutenberg because
movable type made it possible for Eichmann's
captor to convey over time and distance
characteristics of the man more compelling
than rain and beta-carotene and the plaster
cracking beneath my living-room window,
leaving a hole that would otherwise
be an adorable fixation were it not
for pages 199 to 201 of *Eichmann in My Hands*.
This is where Malkin says Eichmann was a very
bad boy who wouldn't eat or move or defecate
until ordered, until his body was returned
to its niche in the chain-of-command, a grid
that braces the stars and provided
all the hands needed to salute the vanishing
of the Jews. This is where the narrative
suddenly turns into a frat movie, Eichmann
in the stall with pajamas at his ankles, asking
                                        May I begin?,
apologizing after each seismic fart, screaming
Entschuldigen Sie, Entschuldigen Sie, convinced
the mingled crimes of gas and constipation
require contrition, an apology for the stench
and frenzy he's added to the human sphere.
Over the course of 71 days I've deleted
thousands of words from this poem, some little
sentences but most long as freight trains,
most striving to list the terrible things
Eichmann did in a way that doesn't sound

like William Conrad or George Kennedy
narrating a PBS documentary, their heads
under water, their heads locked in a vault
to ensure the deep resonance required
when saying *Belsen, Zyklon-B, bodies stacked
like cordwood.* After decades this basso
profundo approach deafens like an all-drum
garage band, like a roof made of hubcaps
terrorized by rain. So I've decided to let Z
represent the quantity of suffering Eichmann
added to the world and admit the quality
of this suffering can't be understood,
an impossibility reminiscent of the koan
about the sound of one hand clapping—
except the hand's been cut off and sleeps
in a pile with other hands. So I've decided
to tell a little joke: what happens
to an agent of the Mossad when an Ober-
sturmführer asks permission to wipe?
The short answer's tears of laughter
and his body doubled over into a question mark.
But if you believe short answers, pi stops
at 3.14 and Neanderthals had big brains
but were really dumb and Bill Thompson's
smile as he beat me with the banana seat
of his Stingray bike is only relevant
in another poem in a galaxy far, far away.
The longer answer ends with Malkin's revelation
some months later, when eating a fig
he realized Eichmann had asked forgiveness
for the sound and smell, for what his body
had to do, but that even with the zero
of the noose closing around his neck,
he'd only apologized for the shit,
for the need and nothing else.

Getting By

Here it is just
Monday, just coffee, just you and fellow workers

of adequate wage
waking up and easing back into doing for others

what you'd not do
for yourselves. A klatch of hardware gurus

advise a neophyte
on the installation of a Sears garage-door opener.

A man in a bolo
struggles between glazed and cream-filled. There is

sun bruising
through windows, converting forms and staplers

and even
the tireless mouth of the Smith & Collier time clock

into spirits,
numinous wells the mind slips down to convert

the papered desk,
the calendar's boast of a woman climaxing over gaskets,

into something
more personal, reveries of sky and water and a smile's

omnipotence.
Just tedium, just fatigue, just you pouring the first

cup and turning
to Wilson and Cartwright and Flynn, all nodding

good morning
until Wilson goes back to fuming about the *sand-nigger*

who cut him
off. Then the confederate lean and laugh, stares tempered

with aspects
of seduction—the mirth of sitcoms, the bonhomie

of beer commercials—
gestures by which your assent is asked and rewarded.

And here you are
smiling back, excusing yourself, sliding to your cubicle

to get down
what the phone wants, what the computer needs, here is self-

loathing, the revenge
of stairway-wit, when suddenly you know the cool, the hard

things to say
about cruelty and desperation and the tribal reflex

to gut every
difference, and shout them, if only in a brave and obsessive

wish. Just you,
just a Monday, just a man in Phoenix begging to get

what he wants
faster, always faster, faster and cheaper than it can possibly

be provided,
and hating you when you tell him the truth. So you lie.

CLAUSEWITZ'S MAIL

An aide found her in a shop in Berlin.
        The offer was five Marks per letter,
two letters per week. She had to be
"scornful of politics and indifferent
to God. Tell her to press hard
so I can touch what I read."
They would never
        knowingly meet. The money, warmed

by the aide's hand, persuaded her to agree.
        That night she stared an hour at a page
before mailing it off blank. Next
she described a man smoking in an arcade,
though there'd been no man, no arcade.
"Tall," she wrote, "his torso hooked,
who paced
        as if waiting for reprieve,

relief from debt or a bad affair.
        I expected him to speak to the air."
These and the next two he left unopened,
stacked on his desk under a stone
lifted from Waterloo. The fifth he read
straight off. "Rain is a conversation.
I've tried
        to measure the intention,

the mood of strangers by the character
        of their stride. Yesterday a man asked
for a bar of soap which smells
'like Istanbul.' I watched a beetle
caught in a web being eaten from inside."
This one he carried to the Ministry of War
and read
        three times during a conference,

enjoying most the line, "Men are smallest
      when they believe themselves responsible
for the horizon." She liked being able
to say anything and so began describing him
to himself. "You enjoy the second but not
the third glass of wine. Under
certain trees
      in the shade of spring you believe

you hear your mother describe
      what the purpose of her shadow is.
Though your left leg's shorter
than your right, you've trained yourself
not to limp." But after two years her last
letter came. "You're assigned
every face
      that appears in my dreams.

It's as if I've wed silence.
      I've decided you're a gentle man. Do not
find me, do not prove me wrong."
Clausewitz burned the letters in an east-
facing room. The cooled ashes he collected
in a tin box, a box he kept by his bed
and touched
      at night before darkness screamed.

THREE FLOORS

On the floor I am more at ease
—Jackson Pollock

God

At St. Michael's on Tuesdays
I knelt on a slate floor, nuns
finding the padding of kneelers
threatening to faith, softer
than Roman nails. The Jew
we killed and claimed slept
on the cross, the brambling crown
slipping across a closed eye
like a hat in a Cagney cock.
We prayed by rote as if listing
Presidents. The discomfort
of kneeling was meant
to be instructive. It was.
I wore knee pads,
eventually converted.

Sex

A back room in the basement, the floor
bed. First bruised then cut, we bled
to fuck, pain an artifact
forming the smaller circles
on our mouths, a stage in the binding
gasp of pleasure. I learned
of the hand that grasps the spine,
the body a shaken tree, the soul
a bronze leaf floating down. The tile
was cool, its pattern Braille,
each square repeating the word
again.

Art

Brushes alienate touch, the relation
of paint to blood. After stretching
the canvas on the floor I work it
on hands and knees, an apostle
feeding by hand, by tongue
the animal the image becomes.
All paintings are portraits,
abstractions of self. Even landscapes
are internal, thoughts
reconstructed as colors and shapes,
made beautiful for the astonishment
of walls. I am in my paintings
more than life, a small sadness,
a price. There's filth in the body's
vanishing, a bond each breath confirms.
I have become the light that clings
to the back of mirrors. What
you perceive in my work isn't art
but a pulse.

ALZHEIMER'S

Chairs move by themselves, and books.
Grandchildren visit, stand
new and nameless, their faces' puzzles
missing pieces. She's like a fish

in deep ocean, its body made of light.
She floats through rooms, through
my eyes, an old woman bereft
of chronicle, the parable of her life.

And though she's almost a child
there's still blood between us:
I passed through her to arrive.
So I protect her from knives,

stairs, from the street that calls
as rivers do, a summons to walk away,
to follow. And dress her,
demonstrate how buttons work,

when she sometimes looks up
and says my name, the sound arriving
like the trill of a bird so rare
it's rumored no longer to exist.

A Gardener

She holds a flower today, I can't
tell from a distance which species of sun, left hand
      processionally high

as her right flicks her cane
up to the first step, five more to go and minutes
      until diligence

brings her to the top, the cane
hooked on the knob and flower set on the banister
      as her hands, blooms

of arthritis, surround the knob
and wheedle open the door. I've counted fifteen small
      metal chairs scattered

around seven gardens, numbers
not unlike those on her wrist, not unlike time if we believe
      it has bones we can count

and a soul made temporal by math.
She ministers to colors and earth, pulls weeds and picks
      out twigs, snips

and breaks away the liabilities
of dying stalks and blossoms, the slow work of a body
      fulfilling prophecy,

a summons to thrive despite
the logical obstacles. What was done to her parents, her family,
      was perversely logical:

this is not said. Nor
do we often say how exquisitely it worked, entire names,
      almost a people vanished,

almost a universe turned to ash
and ash to lies. Sometimes her neighbor comes over and slaps
        a book that says

nothing happened, the ovens
were for bread, the chambers to kill lice, flesh cleansed,
        flesh sanctified.

Sometimes boys speed by
in the booming melancholy of their cars and yell *heeb*
        or *kike*, a ceremony

she contests with the dignity
of beauty, the midwife's tenacity before the demands of each
        tiny birth. I watch

her inching, stooped advance,
the slow turn of wrist that uncorks a weed from its hold,
        knowing creation went

from speck to parsec in a quicker
breath, that an hour of my work's more fertile than her week,
        how her feeble limbs

are signs of her tenuous mind,
thoughts distracted, misdirected as vines. Yet every time
        I see her bend

to the earth's open mouth,
her smile inadvertent, meant for no one, disc of her sun hat
        eclipsing and then

proclaiming her face, I'm moved
to set down the book or dish or crisis I find so crucially
        enticing, and pretend

her life is mine, that I've ceased
wanting more than I'm prepared to understand and have nurtured
        revenge into elegant survival.

WHAT WE SAY

Another poem about a punch press. Another
litany of the line, horizontal inferno,
where steel goes flat to shaped to pierced

in mantric iterations and at a cost to souls.
Another ode to Dewar's and methamphetamines,
to the importance of certain men,

anointed women who provide caps, vials,
a syringe at the right moment
and glowing, light adoring the fluid,

turning it beatific, something out of Vermeer,
Man Shooting-up at a Urinal. Another revelation
of the Talmudic scholar, Descartes fiend

in coveralls, un-degreed prodigy of hyper-
fluid states who for kicks
does virtual crosswords while hunched over a lathe.

Another satire of the love-fest between class
and race, how the Klan and Brothers
of Black Harmony are planning a picnic,

how Capital and Labor are going steady, a bit
of monetary heavy petting, a goo-goo eyed
desire to grant every frivolous wish

of the beloved Other. Another admission
of pride, the epiphany of hands,
of bodies caught in manufacturing's flow,

how despite the abiding cruelties of process
the hood, the tie-rod, the widget
sometimes rises before the ego as totem,

the object created a minor testament
to the vanishing self. *Hard on the land*
wears the strong sea... another proletarian,

and the sun at work every day, greeting us,
Druids all, with quotidian variations
of itself, each sunset the same in different ways.

Another poem about the things we build
that glow and disappear, and the words
we repeat, owning at least what we say.

SELLING MAGRITTE'S HOUSE

The train in the fireplace
stays, immutably bound for Paris or Istanbul. Think of it
as a conversation piece
of industrial muscle, an urban metaphor
offsetting the mantel's
rural chic.
Upkeep's tax-deductible.

A rock in the den's not
so bad. A little imagination, some hardware, a deft
use of explosives
and you've got yourself a lamp. A solid
style, very Ethan Allen,
and what doesn't go
with black? Notice the sky

living inside these windows,
an animal caged in glass. You can tell the owner's
a closet optimist
by the utopian clouds, the comforting drug
of blue. With these,
the mountains
in the next room, the sea

he keeps out back, you've got
an unvarying version of nature, a good investment, hedge
against inflation.
People despise the persecution of change.
Constancy: they'll pay
big-time for that.
The owner? A very regular man,

takes his potatoes boiled,
eyes gouged out, likes to walk his bowler same time
each night, but shy,
a congenital mumbler. He's got a knack

for finding holes
in the horizon,
holds his best conversations

with the backs of heads.
He likes you, says you're different from the others,
admires how you carry
your feet in your hands, your ability
to stand two places
at once. When
I told him you didn't ask

if the howitzer in the den
could be moved but inquired if the deal included shells,
he curled his toes
and smiled. Act soon and I think he'll throw in
his pet bird, its
granite wings
a joke played on the air.

LYONS AVENUE

Ramesh, Ice-T dripping from headphones,
walks the foot-long gash in his back
around the block. Gently tendriled,
butterscotch against hazel skin, the scar's
the map of a river cutting a country
in two. Houses simmer with vacuums
and chatter, the subdued Morse code
of a distant hammer. Ramesh smiles
at sunlight, bounces a tennis ball
just out of reach of the oaks.
When I told him the stuff of Reeboks
and hair and CDs came from stars,
he said *noooo* as if the word's a knot
to be carefully undone. He was holding
the piece of his rib the surgeon
gave him, showing me where it went
when he was whole, child of the *Visible Man*
stiffed by this trinket after asking
for the flattened slug. He waves
as if washing glass, hard and fast
as he burrows into the next moment,
his life, this summer day, pure reflex,
a koan I can't crack. By the time
I wave back a Camry's taken the corner,
the bass of "Two Hard Muthas" shaking flesh
with impenetrable confidence. From behind
a dumpster, Ramesh stares at the gold-
tinted windows floating by, waits,
strides out after the plausible
menace passes, his affection given back
to the sky, the air touching his skin
with endless devotion. Soon all I see
over the ramparts of a neighbor's fence
is the ball going up, coming down,
though I know it hangs for a moment
in space, a time too brief
to believe by any measure but faith.

ALWAYS

CIRCLING THE FLOWERS

No, really, I can't stand it anymore.
If things aren't altered I'll tear my eyes out.
—T.C.

1

So this must be a mouth,
      he thought, bandages off

and the surgeon before him,
          the white of the robe

like the sound of a train
            up close, the color

of hammering, his hand
               finding the surgeon's smile

by the trail of his voice,
                  the abrasion of the once

impossible words, Look
              at me.

2

He could spend an hour
trying to recognize a note

in his own hand—*Mother,*
I woke with the same headache,

pulled the shades, slept
in a chair—but until

he touched the rickety letters
he couldn't read or see

51

his flesh in the curves
and abrupt stops, the splotches

where he'd crossed out, tried
again. He could spend a day

hoping to accept the horizon,
astounded as he moved that it

walked away, how contrarily
an inch-high tree grew

with approach, its
clouded shape becoming a hive

of individual leaves,
the difficulty of overcoming

the old thought that green's
a synonym for smooth.

He could spend only minutes
with his face: the pastiche

reflection caused a temporal
thrashing like furious

bees, the details foreign,
the whole an impossible

accomplishment, no easier
than trying to find language

by a study of lips and teeth
and tongues. After the first

assault of a mirror he slept
two days, dreamed he'd a face

made of water, woke convinced
he'd never been who he was.

3

One day. For one day walls
       made sense, he was able to aim
wine into a glass, even light

in his brother's prism
       served a cathartic function, a river
torn to shreds. It was

two years after the operation,
       cataracts stripped, the surgeon's
paper the talk of Boston,

both of them invited
       to the best parties. On that day
he woke not questioning

sight: the visible
       was normal—window, razor and bed,
the clock's roving arms,

the Sargent on the wall,
       portrait of a military face, the will
for war, a grandfather

he'd never seen except in voice,
       the grind of his adamant syllables.
He wrote to a cousin

in Chicago:*I understood
       today the sun's far away. Shadows
are the souls of bodies*

trying to escape, to lead
        the life of animals. With one finger
I traced the silhouette

of a pineapple on the sill,
        never confusing myself with the shape.
One day, a peace like

the single note of a clarinet
        after it's passed, the void behind sound
not even fear can inhabit.

4

They wouldn't let him touch the painting.
He began to scream, to believe
        that his body was vanishing,
                that the floor was made
of a gauze tapestry, the marble
porous, his hands the webbing of spiders.

The guard clubbed him as he screamed,
thinking him mad, a danger to the ladies
        circling with parasols tucked
                beneath unburdened arms.
        The painting was flat, his eyes
rolled off its edge to the flat walls,

the flat man in the flat bowler standing
beside the painting, even his thoughts flat,
        his mind squeezing to nothing,
                perception compressing
        all history, the notion of his name
and sound of his voice, condensing his life

to a single moment and that moment to a point
that never was, could not
        have been, only his screams
                possessing depth, only the sting
        of the club palpable, reassuring
like a whisper giving shape to an invisible room.

5

Every mirror smashed, the windows
tar-papered.
        The note: *I've circled a vase*
                of tiger lilies for an hour.
They make no sound, their eloquence
        denied me. The more I see

the less I exist. At least blind I lived
inside the world.
        He waited until his family
                was in Maine, the housekeeper
on holiday. He drank three bottles
        of chardonnay, stripped,

took the scissors and sat in a corner.
To bleed
        through the eyes would take
                hours, the coroner wrote.
The priest, refusing burial, asked
        cruelly, What is suicide

but blindness for the will of God?
The body
        was burned without words.
                On a cloudless night
his family fed his ashes to the black
        tongue of the Charles.

A POLITICAL VISION

A cellist in every lobby by love and law.
Even men with crows for eyes stop gnawing
the backs of necks when shouldering
through doors they're swathed
in plaintive air. It's good for the republic.
Like wine in ceremonious amounts—no—half
that, an eighth of what vigorous burghers
consume at weddings, the equivalent
of a finger dipped into a glass and lowered
into the mouth of a child—exactly
that much pleasure, that much sleep.
We tried violin and oboe, jazz sextets,
contrapuntal readings of Brecht by choirs
of Merit Scholars. Machetes were still
being drawn. Now this: the serenity
of elms in moonlight. Even failure
is work, even fatigue deserves its score.
Fauré's Elegy dragged through clouds
of marble: the sensation of breath
bleeding out, hands gripping the rungs
of a sand ladder. And Bach, Suite 6,
allemande—as if every note
came from the knees, a hinge
to be bartered with, that must be asked
to sustain. Even on days when nothing
does, the mist of sound meanders,
shafts toward the woozy floors
where emotions are priced and assigned
spokesmodels. Hobbled instrument,
one-legged and leaning, accommodated
between the thighs, the cello nearly flesh,
essentially vocative. Like it knows names,
all of them, any we might invent,
and that what we feel comes from a hollow
that would moan if bowed.

LETTING GO

If it were a contained explosion, yes, an orderly
breakdown. If the extent to which my head

flew apart or chest imploded could be reversed
in time for supper, absolutely. If it were just

one night in the doorway of a bookstore with
my possessions in seven two-ply bags,

if I could stand up the next morning, dust off,
put on a tie and wing tips and make my way

to the office, complaining on the subway about taxes
to no one in particular in a conspiratorial

tone of voice, I'd happily consent. If I could lose it
in small ways, perhaps only when I'm in the basement,

perhaps while holding the sander but not the drill,
certainly there'd be limited access to fire, maybe

the city could set aside a field for lunatic purposes,
for tirades and fits, something like a carnival

where you approach a man whose eaten several-hundred-
too-many corn dogs and give him a little

red ticket, in this case to enter a space
bounded by an electric fence, in this case

to pull hair, your own or the sweat-matted locks
of dentists and jugglers, to eat and worship dirt,

scream in mimicry of bone-snap and buzz saw,
make a house of your blackest thoughts

and chew it to dust board by board, liking nails
best. Of course I'd rather eat sandwiches

beside the open mouth of the ocean
or recover from my tendency

to dispute even the simplest gestures
of kindness and need. But when I sit

at the table afraid of sunlight or hide
behind the couch because a man's at the door,

I feel the proximity of something denser, that if
someone dear died, if a tree looked at me

the wrong way or the bones of a clerk's face
revealed themselves for a second, a white flash,

a toothy leer, I'd slide into that thicker existence,
begin living inside the drone of cicadas

and asking strangers to describe their most
hated sensation with knives on my skin. I hold on

by painting the walls whiter each year, more
like the inside of the sun, stare at words

on a screen and believe they make something tangible,
a weaving I can wrap around my shoulders

that says *fuck you* to the wind. Perhaps
I'd let go if the needles were tufted, if

I could chew on my limbs in a bloodless way,
say what I mean without dismantling my face

and drift off the ledge with the knowledge
that in that moment I'd understand one thing

so perfectly it would die with me—I would
not, not even then, not even with a guarantee

of worship by similarly inclined fools. As if
I'd be asked, as if I'd see it coming

and be able to duck, say no thank you, not now—
as if it's a choice I'll make like the style

of suit I'll wear to the doctor's when I explain
that the voice is always there and strangely comforting.

ABSENCE

There are men and women huddled in rooms tonight
discussing dark matter, the non-stuff, the anti-
things that fill the universe. Imagine writing
that grant. Their children are of relatively
specific dimension, their houses occupy
nearly calculable space. Seven have dogs.
One dreams of playing in the British Open
nude. Yes, exactly like your father.
Of special interest is the woman in an office
in Princeton in a swivel chair looking
through a window at the pond where Einstein's
said to have sat and thought about sailboats,
the little ones German children race on Sundays.
She whispers *Bolivia*, a word she caught
on a map earlier and hasn't been able to shake.
She has never been there. She has never left
the east, finds Bar Harbor exotic, thinks
of lobsters as the first wave of an alien invasion.
Together with a colleague she is trying to total
the mass of everything, the mental equivalent
of 27 clowns cramming into a '60s vintage Volvo.
What she likes about the word Bolivia
beside the sexual things it does to the tongue
is her feeling that anything you do there
might cause people to dance. She would like
to dance now. If most of what exists
can't be seen or spread on toast
or wedged under a door in summer
when you want to fall asleep on the couch
to a wind that began somewhere near Topeka,
it's acceptable to dance on a desk in an office
paid for by the Rockefeller Foundation
in an attempt to resurrect that once
good name. And even as she pictures herself
clearing and scaling the desk,
she is striding to the board and brushing

away a series of calculations
and replacing them with another, more
elegant run, adding at the end the curlicue
of infinity, which normalizes the equation,
which makes her noodling momentarily right
with God and explains how a pinhole
could have the density of a universe, how half
of Jupiter could lie balled in your shoe.
Bolivia, she says, spinning. Bolivia,
she repeats, grabbing Bill Morrison
by the collar. Bolivia, he answers,
embracing the odd particulars of revelation,
kissing her hand in a burlesque of manners,
knowing it's just made chalk beautiful,
aligned the glyphs of mass and spin
into a schematic of everything. Then briefly,
looking over his shoulder at the board,
she realizes in essence she's trapped
nothing, not the stars but the black leading
between the light, the same absence
she feels at night when looking up a force
like wind rises through her body, leaving
no trace except the need to be surrounded
by anything more comforting than space.

MEMORIAL DAY

Each year my parents flowered their dead: the dark-veined
        geraniums, blue fog of Russian sage
        ritual impregnations. I carried trowels
and loppers, collected limbs my father hacked. He liked

to groom oak and maple, tidy their shadows,
        the green recklessness an outrage
        against the middle class. Families
are like weeds: spreading conquers. We had four cemeteries

to visit, at this only covering basics, parents and aunts,
        uncles and greats, their families
        too big to comfort the lesser deities.
We'd drive with the radio off, my mom looking back

time to time, asking if I remembered this-or-that relation,
        telling me where they'd lived,
        when they'd died, how the names
and genes of our clan got knit, a catechism of souls.

The land was meditative, a theme grudging slight variations:
        Holsteins clumped on one farm,
        scattered on another, this barn door
open, that coop falling down, a copse occasionally, once

a stand of red pine all blown the same direction, leaning
        away from history's storm. Suddenly
        we'd pull beneath an iron arch—
Chattleford Memorial, Bethlehem Acres—onto a patch of grass

struggling toward green, the dead in rows neat as crops. We'd
        unload, I'd work an hour, then wander
        among the stones, reading names and dates,
questioning claims of modesty, temperance and forbearance,

morsels of spin-control thought devotional. Curious
       as I was, I feared trampling heads
       and hands, that some essence
remained sensate, would be pissed, vengeful if stomped.

I trod judiciously as Wallenda. By the time I got back
       they'd have clipped around the marker
       of a Hicok or Fineis or Finch,
have brushed the dirt and grass away, watered the buoyant

mouths of flowers and assayed a bit of telepathy with dust
       and God. Later I learned the scum
       some of these people were, adulterous,
petty, one prone to beat whatever moved, a singularity of hate

terminated by a slug, a case even the sheriff zealously
       dropped. It didn't matter:
       on Memorial Day all were sainted,
venerated for the accomplishments of breath and memory,

governance of home and thresher, the dual fecundities
       of womb and field. Solitude
       defines this land, you can drive
hours without the intercession of a face, approach

a moon snagged on horizon's saw-toothed trees
       in full confidence
       no other fool in the county's
similarly engaged. My parents never said anything

about loving these people: reticence is in the blood: love's
       acted, not said. It's the work
       of hands, the carnal gift of bloom,
the beauty entrusted to graves a sensual payment of debt.

Rothko's Last Meditation

In the days leading to the miracle he did not
bathe or speak, ate
only bread and oranges and slept on the floor
under a window
covered by a sheet of moonlight. Vines grew
through the house.
On each leaf the face of a child appeared
and aged
through adolescence and adulthood, finally death
as the leaves curled
into small red fists. The first to vanish
were neighbors
and the man who sat on his stoop playing a drum
with the obsession
of rain eating at land. An hour after their bodies
disappeared
their shadows followed, absorbed by the ground
which sealed around them
like a mouth. And when their abandoned voices
entered his body
and coalesced, collapsed the way starlight
can fall back upon
and consume itself—when even he had vanished
into that black
pearl of negation, thought and the ravelings of color
ceased. He became a shape
floating above horizon, the world's luminous edge,
and for a moment felt
nothing, a miraculous calm he'd soon lose and chase
into his chosen death.

REUNION

The story's that my great-aunt was killed by her mother
        for having an affair with a married man, some
                toxic concoction slipped into her tea
on a winter day when the wind came sharp as a convert's
revelation of the Lord's unconquerable might. It's still told

at family picnics, usually three beers into rummy
        or at dusk on the beach as fire ravages
                a century of wood, confided to someone's
new girlfriend or the nephew who's begun staring at the tidal
sway of women, an uncle kicking it off, outlining the depth

and color of her wild and unbreakable love before, tag-
        team fashion, my sister or aunt slide in,
                give a flavor to the tea, describe
the little farm painted on the cup, the print of the dress
torn as her body slid to the floor. Stories, more than eye

color, hemophilia, the DNA encoded with a taste for scotch,
        are the genetics of clan, how blood subverts
                the fascism of time, how flesh replicates
the icons and totems through which guilt is ritualized
and absolution gained, how we persuade our children

to wear wing-tips, vote the party line, do the right thing.
        The year one of the living strayed, my cousin
                Randolph caught in his car with a student
flunking Hotel Management, when we gathered just three months
after his wife loaded his Grand Am with the Palmer clubs

and McIntosh stereo and torched it in the drive, we talked
        of the year's slow blooming roses, of baseball,
                that form of collective meditation,
of ways to loosen rusted nuts and cleanse sheets of blood.
They came late and loaded with beer and potato salad,

held hands and smiled for pictures, pitched shoes,
        cooed babies and looked away from the corners
                in which their history was designed,
the details verified and fictionalized, betrayal graphed,
the edges between the acts of forgiveness and retribution

smoothed, the story worked in pockets until by cross-
        pollination the family had decided which
                bloom truth was, after which
there was nothing to say but what in essence we do every year:
how hard we are to love, how desperate to stay together.

TEXTBOOK CASE

> *. . . he made a vow that he would sacrifice a hundred oxen*
> *to the gods if they would grant him a return to health.*
> —from Aesop's *Impostor*

A certain man fell ill. The year of coughing passed
as the year of migraines began. In dreams

a row of doctors in hula skirts lined up and shrugged
as if lifting a mountain. Friends became indifferent

as daffodils. So he read up on haustrum and macula
densa; pyemotes ventricosus, the gravid parasite

burrowing under skin; ectopia testes, the straying
of testicles from the orthodox descent, an image

that kept him awake and pacing, fingers
flitting over his abdomen like the wisp-legs

of Jesus bugs. He began making promises, first
to himself, oaths to eat the foods recommended

by experts with the most iridescent skin, to bathe
in oils extracted from the glands of carnivores

in the hope their chi could navigate pores. Slowly
he involved the sky, began looking at weather

as a supplicant, sought to appease the wallpaper
and bedspread, developed the breakfast habits

of a monk: a ritual buttering of toast, precise
straining of juice, the table set meticulously,

as if by alignment of flatware and condiments
he could direct the god of health his way,

a landing strip of happy-ever-afters. Nothing.
Then good deeds occurred to him, a prescription

of donations and promotions, then lies
and why not, why not say the baby's beautiful,

why not tell each daughter they'll inherit
his knickknacks, his moiety of earth. And after

his breath turned a paint-stripping stench,
after his feet curled in and under, a simian

reconstitution, after gallstones and gout
and hallucinations of fibrous tumors the size

of pomegranates, he gathered 100 oxen, looked
into the seeds of their eyes as he slit 100 throats,

watched their blood bless the field and asked
for health or at least forbearance, a Buddha

disposition if not a martyr's persistence,
if nothing else the good fortune to die.

Choosing My Conception

My mother at a party in a blue dress
dancing, left-handing a Bacardi and Coke in June
as the house pants through open windows.
Two men in the backyard clutching imaginary
nine irons, miming their swings
for the analytical reflections of the moon.
A woman seven months along in a sunflower
muumuu accepting suggestions for names—saints
and ballplayers, a candidate promising Camelot—
as hands shadow her belly, a reflex of memory.
Nancy Sinatra on the hi-fi, my mother employing
more hip, closing her eyes and shimmying
against the base line. Everyone floating
a half inch off the floor, the season
a thermal in the blood making them dream
like hawks, making them crave sky. My mother
dancing with the tide of Todd Rawlings,
with his premonitions, the air he's about
to inhabit. They don't care for each other
the way my father worries, watching
from the flagstone fireplace, Betty Thomas
composing an ode to hydrangeas in his right ear.
They don't touch each other or the lyrics,
don't know the room exists, that dishwashers
are on sale and pillbox hats a must. A little
rum, the heat of a woman finally singing
in her natural register, done
with the virginal songs, the doo-wop
tease. If for three minutes you could vanish
into your knees, into the deepest meat
of your brain, the part that thrums
hosanna, the kernel unharrowed by words,
how readily your bliss might be mistaken
for lust. So despite the shame of something
deeper showing, the unhinged self, my father
comes over between songs, lowers

my mother's head to his shoulder
and begins to sway
rigidly, like rust, until her skin
and the blue dress with one strap
almost falling, until her hands
plowing the long muscles of his back,
make him forget he hates to dance,
to douse his body in music. After an hour
of Ray Charles, Dean Martin and the diesel
of Patsy Cline, my parents leave, walk past
their red Valiant, arms vined across
each other's back, to a park where a bronze man
threatens stars with a saber. And for once
my father's able to say what doesn't
make sense but flows, to articulate
something like rhythm, she's able to forget
what he wants for a second, to look away
from his face at the willows shaking their hair
to attract the moon, suddenly they're both
devoted to the echo of a tune, the strap
of a blue dress falling, and soon,
and randomly I will exist.

PLACE

A speedball at the old college above Olmsted's
terraced garden, maples sloughing leaves
but sumacs hanging on, pyromancers fireworking
end-time. Smoke in his blood like shadows
in a river, black shiver of crows
needling water's silver outbreak.
For the first time in a week the sky's free
of November's customary penance, its woolen
gloom. So the drug feels blue and expansive,
the usual kick of euphoria notched up,
a ratcheting toward god-arrogance, a burst
of possessiveness that gives him
cityscape, foundry smoke, the Cadillac
in the distance hushing A to B as a cloak
of temporary opulence. It's so brief, this
compassion, prelude to thimble-mood,
the whore-implosion he'll feel as he walks
down the hill to the Flamingo or Carl's,
as he readies his face for the charm-lie,
the souvenir of love and exhilaration
he'll grant men who want all resignation
stroked from their bodies. To be reduced
to beauty and beauty to a mouth, to soft,
slender hands and linchpin secrets,
master of the fetishes about which
he never speaks out. Hand job
beneath the glare of Augustus Walker,
Civil War hero. Smell of leather
in the office of First National's president.
His finger tracing the river of a bypass scar
in a hotel room beside the stadium, a roar
in every ghost-throat.
But not in this fond Arcadia. Just pills
or pipe, preparatory buzz, a bit
of pharmacological stiff-upper-lipping
before work. How vast this clear weather becomes,

how precious the marble steps of a school
built to float above a city. As the coke peaks,
the gold ripple of horizon moves closer,
the fading grass levitates, an oddly
restful excitation, his mind feeding
on color. This moment will grow
through the night to what he projects
on the veil of every face—a trick of refusal,
innovation of grunt-mouth and blush
into the unhooded countenance of affection—
making each man, if only for the scope
of one breath, something more
than a doll thrashed by need's reflex.
A skill out of which a myth of change
is fashioned, the possibility of a life
on the Côte d'Azur, of eyes capable
of meeting his in a ritual
more sustaining than panic, bones
to cherish as if unearthing treasure.

A POET

THE ARCH OF SANCTIFICATION

The Arch of Sanctification, St. Louis Cathedral,
depicts the Holy Spirit as a dove in God's chest.

I could use a dove in my heart.
I could use this God of Italian tile,
Lee Marvin in dreadlocks, light surging
from head and hands, Zeus-circuitry
spewing gold and only slightly
less prophetic than St. Louis sun.
Go now, His heart says, and be plain
all your years: Scheherazade awaits.
Go now and live mute among lepers:
their suffering is also song.
Go now and kiss your enemies
hard at the lips like the clasp
of revelation: the taste of malice
is also sacred. You, Holy Spirit,
were the one I never got, a pixie,
to wound the Catholic lexicon,
though without pranks, Trinity's wisp,
carrier of sanctification. Meaning what?
This is the fog the Sisters offered: walls
must be led to faith, stones softened
to belief. This the confounding sincerity
of the Priest: through the Spirit
our poor bones were created. I lower mine
into the creaking music of a pew.
I could use a dove in my heart
because wanting's made it small, no room
for wings or a civil wish. Even now
I want this mosaic, to carry
and adore it to pieces, down to sketch,
down to the artist's hands mapping the tiles,
sweating until he hears the voice of God
and why not. I hear the voice of God
all the time, god of an agnostic, a whisper
that says you must love better, must love

more. I devise the moment's theology:
Spirit's the comfort of vanishing
into the palm of a cathedral
where I'm mixed, part and parcel,
woven back into the father and son,
the word of myself. In an hour
I'll come apart in a hotel room,
bad habits and ice, one window and finally
me in a chair staring at the red lights
of an antenna, writing the list
of whose fault this is. Against that time
I memorize the sweep of wings, let
white feathers stain my eyes.
Saints in designer robes look down,
thin as Byzantium. If I pray
it's to taunt, to beg them to speak.

THE LIFE

The first time I watched he lifted his shirt
to reveal the .45, drew a finger to his mouth
in a gesture of silence and ignored me

until today. Seventy degrees and squirrels
swarming over trees like fluffy maggots, spring
floating up through their blood, making them twist

in the air as if two winds are being reconciled
within their bodies. Torpid glide of cars,
Escorts and Caddys making the pilgrimage

to his drive, today his business conducted
outside, grams and bills passing hands
beneath the improvisation of silver chimes,

a few staying for a beer and toke, smoke
giving the air topography, shapes that molt
into dreams, into nothing. When it was my turn

for such a life I was good at finding veins
and cutting lines, knowing when to smile
like the gates of heaven swinging wide

or touch the handle of a bat, the slow
caress of vengeance. One week
I made five grand on the couch, saying yes,

saying no, whispering numbers to the phone
while Billy flitted between the windows,
interrogating both light and dark

for what didn't belong, shaking and promising
to graduate from the next high into detox.
When I came home from getting baggies and beer

to find Billy separated from himself, the blast
up close, I was half an hour from the airport
and four days in New Orleans finishing

everything I had, half an hour and four days
from sitting in a wicker chair and staring
at the ocean, convinced it was breathing,

that the land was sweating and soon to open
its mouth. I watch my neighbor like anyone
whose done a certain job and moved on, hands

sensitive to the gestures, mind alert in
unexpected ways, how I can still tell
from a distance if there's something in a sock,

by the quaver in a voice if what's really
being said isn't *What's up* but *motherfucker*.
Neighbors talk about burning him out or blowing

him up, pet their shotguns as if they'd scatter
what scares them like a puff on a dandelion.
Today in this fine weather I watch

as he fades into the corner of his porch,
white skin eclipsed by shadow, a man habitually
invisible. When he leans out and points

a finger my way, it's with an arrogance
I'd forgotten, the high of living
with the faith you know precisely how you'll die.

ONE THING AND ANOTHER

The crows are tagged to see how far they'll take
the night of their bodies. Five big as miniature
dachshunds own the oak and the air they've filled
with backfire. I ask my friend who farms if crows
kill or just scavenge. This reminds him he saw
a hawk hunt a blue jay above the red pine
three men can hug without touching fingers.
The hawk landed on a branch with the jay limp
as rope in its mouth. Crows he doesn't think
hunt or pick on other birds as jays do.
He hates jays as the bullied must and tells me
four boys sealed him in the closet of a half-
built house with cinder blocks when he was 8
and he was there most of the night. Two of them
still live down the road and recently asked
if he'd help with the threshing and at the end
of the day one of them mentioned what happened
and smiled as if remembering his first erection.
The crows fly off and come back like there's a wind
inside they're trying to let out. I ask why he helped
and he says his father had a cow that hated
the cold and got sick more often than the others.
Once it slipped on some ice and five bulls
circled, kicked and butted until it was bleeding
everywhere and his father shot it in the head
with a .38, the sound from his bed like a roll
of caps pounded with a rock. He asks
if I think crows are ugly and I say I used
to wander the abandoned Vernor's plant, adoring
the ghost machines as a priest might robes
and chalices and blood wine. Everything the crows
say is rust and we listen to them hate
our presence until they fly off with the red
wounds of their tags. I ask if his mother
still shoots them out of her swamp-white oak.
He says she sleepwalks and last month

he found her beside the grave of her husband,
night coat open, black birds beginning
their soothsaying, her hair too wild not to stroke
before waking her to a face she made long ago
out of something irreparable as love.

FAITH IN SFAKIA

—

Old women in furnaces of black muslin dresses
shadow kiosks and cafés, shawled and answering

the call to prayer along cobblestones
etched by the paths of their devotion.

—

The listening of God is not a temporal act.

—

Elana Rodotus, twisted by fever into a vine,
has risen. Four days thrashing, speaking

to bodies that have left the room, stepped
off the edge of the terraced night,

vanished into the vow of death. Remnants
of the candles her daughter burned

stare with black eyes. She's strong enough
for broth. On the cross, a blissful

Jesus looks up. The priest had come, sanctioned
the silence of her flesh, absolved her

of the quest for innocence. Today the word miracle
is whispered across the lips of spoons.

—

The cemetery's fenced, its filigreed iron
painted black, the paint flecked,

a Victorian high-collar around death's thin neck.
Granite and marble crosses, the *ts*

of an enervated alphabet, and glass-topped,
steel-plate boxes filled

with artifacts that speak for the dead: brass
dice, two packs of Karelia, crescent wrench,

porcelain rabbit, statue of the Virgin placed
on a letter postmarked Madrid,

each sustaining a mind's reputation, the need
of hands for ponderable burdens.

—

Prayer focuses the will of God. The women
chastise by plea, shape their hands

into caves and fill the caves with a wind
of names and names. Because no man

believes what he does is evil, the women believe
every hand, each eye is the premonition

of a weapon. In the center of town, 39 skulls
smile in their reliquary, 39

bullet holes, the mouths of 39 moons. In every
hand a war, in each eye the eroticism

of fire. The will of God is vague and distracted.
A wind of names and names.

—

Bent knees, the knots of the rosary thumbed,
each voice kneading words,

the gathering of voices a flock of birds. Widows
and mothers, the scent

of husbands and daughters weighting their fingers,
centuries of bone, a way

of speaking which is a premonition of the air.
Saint Nicholas watches the children

who walk the mountains, Saint Peter hovers
above the men who fish with dynamite.

Each day a blue wheel, each night a bright emotion.
Sometimes the children fall

into the mouth of the world, sometimes the men do not
come back. Their bones undo, loosen

into light. It's light these women pray to,
doubting the myth of bodies,

believing the island floats on water pooled
in the hand of God. Seven

times a day they come, matins to compline. A clock
is made of their walking, the black

ticking of their strides. One thousand years
have passed like this

or one second, one thousand years that weigh no more
than a leaf to the sky.

THE CORONER'S REPRIEVE

*We report two cases of asphyxiation during autoerotic
activity employing hydraulic shovels on tractors.*
                    —Journal of Forensic Sciences

For the third time in a week he dreams
he wears the scarf, black silk,
excretion of worms.

He blushed when he saw the body,
stood behind the barn
until soothed by the sea-sway of wheat in wind.

The scarf, knotted to the end
of a rope tied to the front-loader's bucket,
had to be cut from the dead man's
neck, severing
the painted white moon from the snare
of mountains.

He'd read of this, heard two men at a convention
in Memphis debate the spin
it would give an orgasm, fear
and the loss of oxygen
compounding ecstasy.

Tonight
for a breath after waking he doesn't recall
his wife has died,
begins to form her name
but remembers, says it
anyway.

In the dream a man cuts his body down
from a tree, touches him
with hands made of water, turns his eyes around
in his head and buries him,
commenting he's no longer a danger to anyone.

The dead man wore nylons,
a garter, his neck was scarred, his hand and penis
callused, details the coroner
typed on paper and slipped into a blue file.

He's clothed in his dream, hangs without choking,
dies calmly,
as if pouring tea.

Tonight, wrapped in a quilt,
he stares at the houses, imagines them dogs
sleeping, curled
around the oracles of their hearts.

There was a sky in the dead man's face, November
gray, his feet were balloons
of blood.

Shame was all the coroner felt then,
ridiculous even touching him,
though now he thinks of him as brave, valuing
a moment beyond logic
or pride, ingenious with his lust, determined
enough to die.

INERTIA

There he was with Galileo, measuring the speed
of stones, cutting cannonballs
in half and clocking the pieces in their fall.

Scooter's bark snapped his head from the book
to a sugar maple,
four shades of red, dwindling green. The dog

wagging at his foot, yipping like a jammed
machine, wanting out
to root among junipers and bulbs and nag

the clamorous breathing of neighbors. Placing
the open book
pages down, a tent of the slow, sensual progression

of reason, he frowned at the dog and shuffled
toward the back door, trying
to memorize a dead man's notion *that physical bodies*

have physical inclination to some motion,
liking the idea
that desire is manifest in wing-tips and clocks.

There was no thought in his change of direction,
the sudden spin
toward the front door, or malice or joy

in watching the dog shoot out, cut across the lawn
and disappear
into the mouth of Thompson Park, leashless,

unfenced for the first time in its life. Later, after
Scooter's demise
beneath the radial tire of a Blazer, he shrugged

along with his wife and son, asked if they knew
how he got out,
sincerely moved by their grief but needing to lie

for once about something other than how he feels,
to claim a material
deception. Alone that night on the couch,

reading the same sentence—*and therefore, all external*
impediments removed . . .
time and again, he realized it was confidence he felt

as he pushed the door open, and a sense of relief
he could let
such a wild, such a cruel thing happen.

YOUR FATHER DEAD

—for J.F.

Your father dead and a field to mow.
            Corn filling another, twenty acres of green-
            sheathed sun. Your boy
                        up the night with croup, a buckshot
cough. A maple's
            storm-sheared limbs to be sealed.

Your father dead and mother alone.
            She calls late, asks when he's coming home.
            The meals you bring
                        she gives to the cats, twelve strays
that never left.
            Last week, handing up

an iced tea as you sat on the Deere,
            she suddenly said he was hollow by the end,
            as if finishing
                        a conversation you couldn't hear.
You worried her
            across the road. Your father dead

and wife concerned. She says you spin
            more than sleep, don't walk so much as dream
            through rooms, a ghost
                        with b.o. She recommends
you go to his stone
            and have your say, knowing men

are usually late, better
            at never. Your father dead and you now father.
            Your son weighs no more
                        than the words he butchers,
you carry him
            as if holding a river. What

you owe him fills your mind,
        bread and stories, your poor cache of wisdom.
        Worry's instinctual,
                a reflex of the body's devotion.
Except his smile
        nothing's certain. Your father dead

and a field to mow.
        The Merc's transmission's shot. Work's
        where you go, haven
                and submission. This
is what he taught
        but secretly hoped you'd outgrow.

SERVICE

In the hospital he moans he was wrong, insists through delirium
        the spirit hadn't moved on him the way
          he'd thought. Clyde Dawkins shook the box tonight, closed
    his eyes and reached in, let head or tail come,

held the rattler before his face and began preaching against the tide
        of filth, the pollution of the body delivered
          to bliss. *They shall take up serpents; and if they drink*
    any deadly thing, it shall not hurt them.

Stu Wallace beat a tune out of his guitar, a penitential music,
        kicked his good foot against the side
          of the stage and stared at the shadow of the Lord as it slid
    across Clyde. August in Kentucky, shirts with their half-moons

of sweat, the women's hair piled into blond and red pagodas.
        To believers, everything palpable's
          ordained. The misery of the man who owned this gas station,
    who shot himself in Nashville and willed the property

to Roberta Devins, first row, head back and singing *He's God*
        in Alabama, He's God in Tennessee.
          The guilt of Ray Chandler, whose fingers harass the piano,
    who often dreams of a boy with his pants down,

the boy's smile a gate. And Clyde's hands, Clyde's face, his body
        offered to a faith sacrificial at its core,
          that looks beyond rosary and Bible, beyond water and blood,
    beyond the eyes of Jesus staring down from the cross—

who forgave the act but not the joy of crucifixion—and worships
        ecstasy, pain coiled with pleasure,
          and wants a man to take up snakes, to handle the Angel of Death
    and survive, and fail prophetically. Tonight the snake spun

and struck, the forty-third time Clyde's been bitten, a number
        Loreen Eliston converts to seven, *Seven*
          angels who had seven plagues. Before sleeping he grips
    his wife's hand, repeats he was at fault, a blindness

to the will of Jesus. In the waiting room she reports to the massed
        congregation, tells the eleven souls
          Clyde will be fine, repeats what he said and notes that facts
    conform to scripture, for though he writhes he breathes

God's air. And after praying they discuss next week, decide when
        they'll meet, who'll bring the snakes,
          who'll mix the strychnine from which they'll sip, sewing up
    the practical details of their faith.

NONSTOP

Did you notice the herding instinct of grief?
That as the woman drifted from the tunnel
of the plane, she and the box of ashes
in her hands were absorbed in a midnight
of topcoats? These questions are unethical
because you weren't there. This is a crime
between me and my God, who is shorter
and a better cook than your God. I often
feel I'm waiting for God at the airport
because people disembark with the sky
branded to their faces. Only God can do this:
only Stephen Hawking knows how. So you weren't
there but I was, waiting for a woman
who might not love me anymore, who coveted
mystical experiences in the desert and knew
scorpions are rare in Chicago and New York.
Did you realize you can talk so long to a woman
in Brooklyn that your body in Elgin
gets confused with the Anglo-Saxon words
we use to express deep emotion? This
is a fairer question because if you're older
than one you've wanted something
with an intensity that vibrates skin.
So even though you weren't there you know
my body fluttered in its wishing, the hope
she'd arrive with smile and kisses, as a voice
on the PA preaching a change of heart
and the everlasting covenant of our flatware.
Mostly I was meditating on my smaller sorrow
when interrupted by vast lamentation,
little sobs that grew in pitch
to the screams of fierce machinery
breaking down in the throat. Mostly
I forgot the bad breath of planes
because of the woman and ashes, because
the black fog of bodies absorbed her body,

took her inside their grief as we want
to go inside a house, a room, a bed
and the dream of water that lives within
the bed, waiting for our sleep to unleash it.
My God says these were not seven people
but one, joined in reverence
for what fire subtracts from ash,
but my God won't fight your God on this.
My God will make pasta fagioli for your God,
who should bring the wine. My God
will keep me awake with guilt for contrasting
the loss of love to the loss of the loved
body. But as the grieving moved off
without moving apart, a little country
shifted through Concourse D by a private
tectonics, I wanted such a clutter of flesh
around me, to cling to arms and the scent
of hair, the scent of bodies breaking down
the frail perfumes. When the woman I love
softly touched my back and spoke my name
like an egg breath could crack, I knew
we'd spend the weekend thinking of rain
falling elsewhere, of moonlight
shining up through the bottom of the earth,
everything said sounding like glass
softly hammered in a bag. Returning her
to the airport on Sunday, I had only my God
for solace, who wails for no one, whose flesh
is useless words.

FIELDWORK

There are two kinds of people and five hundred
seventy-one thousand, three hundred
ninety-six species of beetle but who's
counting? Technically a small tribe
concerns itself with this number and the colors
and types of jaws that make up this number,
like my friend who returned from months
in the treetops of the Amazon with a fever
and a jar and a beetle that looked like Jimmy
Durante. She's one of the two kinds
of people and I'm one of the other
so we get along very well providing we don't
tie our bodies into a position that leads
to dilated pupils and the shared
obsession of a self-cleaning lint trap.
By the time she got off the plane the fever
had her saying things about milk
and rayon and Mr. Magoo that make
as much sense as a harpsichord played
with an anvil. This led to my driving
in a way that proved you can be
in two places at the same time
and to the removal of plastic coverings
from innumerable plastic devices
the doctors knew reflexively
how to use and a few days of her face
imitating the maps of clouds
they show us each night on TV as the one
kind of person she is
tried not to die. When something
like spring came back into her hands
and the flower of a sound
rose from her tongue it was the word
jar, which she repeated until I found
the cylinder with its yellow liquid
and little tank-body of a beetle floating

like Michelangelo painted it
on the same day he finished the finger of God
as it lazed toward the finger of Man.
And everything that would come
later, the taxonomy and papers
and extension of her grant, had nothing
to do with her gratitude toward the jar
and the black and red, the fierce creature
inside, which she set on her pillow
and touched from time to time to remind
her body of its life in the trees. Maybe
there are seven kinds of people and three
kinds of beetle and two
delicatessens where you can get a fried-
tuna sandwich on waffles but only one
reason she was back in the Amazon just
two months later writing in her small
script that looks like cuneiform
run through a blender. And if your sanity's
too highly calibrated or you wear
slippers to get to your shoes or need
to label the drawer in which you keep
your labeler, you're probably not
the kind of person who'll understand
sleeping in the green canopy of frenzied
sounds with nets strung about you
and a harness around your body because every
kind of person eventually must fall
but how many
get to touch and name and adore
a fraction and flutter of life not even
the jealous eyes of God have seen?

THANKSGIVING

Today I sided with the sleepwalkers. Today
I believed the moon is my grandmother and I
am an echo of the moon. She looked
small enough to bathe in a teacup, frail
as a tree that's eaten every gale but now
has no teeth for the next wind. She lived
between sleep and wakefulness
much as the souls of purgatory are neither
here nor there. It's what she said
and the drowsiness of her repetitions,
her ability to look through my body and address
the horizon as me. I can't tell you
what she meant because the pilgrimage she made
with the devotion of her phrases escaped
my simple grasp of mortality. She spoke
of home, about coming to and losing it, listed
every place she's lived and paid
loving tribute to the daughters and sons
who moved the La-Z-Boys and brought
potato salad to christen the double-wide.
There was a town in Iowa where a cow
was elected mayor, a berg in Washington
where it rained enough to satisfy
the carpenter in Noah. In every stop
her husband was still alive and planting
rutabagas or adjusting a carburetor.
In every kitchen there were Jell-O molds
of stars and trout, as if the body
of a fish should always wiggle and have
an appetite for light. In every memory
there was something deeper, a hidden fact,
a date that must be rendered exact,
she went back and said it wasn't
red, wasn't '66 but '65, June instead
of August and not the best surprise
of the year but maybe her life

when she realized the sun would rise
on her new
kitchen table every morning
until she died. What I get wrong doesn't
matter because she wasn't talking to me
or even herself or even the God
she believes in with the certainty
I once had that the white shirts
in my closet were ghosts that breathed
come night. The sleepwalkers
know this desk is a dream and my hands
fluttering across the keyboard are what
crows long ago decided I should say.
The moon and my grandmother have made
their peace. I felt its pull
when I bent to kiss her cheek good-bye,
its dust on my lips in the car as I stared
at fields in which the premonition
of wheat loomed as a story the farmers
cannot wait to tell.

OTHER LIVES AND DIMENSIONS AND FINALLY
A LOVE POEM

My left hand will live longer than my right. The rivers
        of my palms tell me so.
Never argue with rivers. Never expect your lives to finish
        at the same time. I think

praying, I think clapping is how hands mourn. I think
        staying up and waiting
for paintings to sigh is science. In another dimension this
        is exactly what's happening,

it's what they write grants about: the chromodynamics
        of mournful Whistlers,
the audible sorrow and beta decay of *Old Battersea Bridge*.
        I like the idea of different

theres and elsewheres, an Idaho known for bluegrass,
        a Bronx where people talk
like violets smell. Perhaps I am somewhere patient, somehow
        kind, perhaps in the nook

of a cousin universe I've never defiled or betrayed
        anyone. Here I have
two hands and they are vanishing, the hollow of your back
        to rest my cheek against,

your voice and little else but my assiduous fear to cherish.
        My hands are webbed
like the wind-torn work of a spider, like they squeezed
        something in the womb

but couldn't hang on. One of those other worlds
        or a life I felt
passing through mine, or the ocean inside my mother's belly
        she had to scream out.

Here, when I say *I never want to be without you,*
        somewhere else I am saying
I never want to be without you again. And when I touch you
          in each of the places we meet,

in all of the lives we are, it's with hands that are dying
          and resurrected.
When I don't touch you it's a mistake in any life,
          in each place and forever.

ACKNOWLEDGMENTS

I'd like to thank the editors of the following publications, whose judgment was sufficiently impaired to accept these poems:

Black Warrior Review	"One Thing Certain," "Circling the Flowers," "Letting Go," "Thanksgiving"
Boulevard	"Absence," "Inertia"
Chelsea	"A Gardener," "Faith in Sfakia"
DoubleTake	"Lyons Avenue"
Epoch	"Three Floors"
Farmer's Market	"Choosing my Conception"
Fine Madness	"Place"
Indiana Review	"Heroin"
Iowa Review	"Over Coffee," "The Coroner's Reprieve"
The Journal	"One Thing and Another," "Nonstop," "Other Lives and Dimensions and Finally a Love Poem"
The Kenyon Review	"Waiting for UPS"
Michigan Quarterly Review	"Selling Magritte's House"
Poetry	"Rothko's Last Meditation"
Poetry East	"Getting By"
Poetry Northwest	"Louise," "Superstition," "Clausewitz's Mail," "The Arch of Sanctification"
Prairie Schooner	"Textbook Case"
Shenandoah	"Plus Shipping," "Watching Welles"
The Southern Review	"Alzheimer's," "A Political Vision"
Tar River Poetry	"Memorial Day," "Reunion," "Service"
Witness	"The Applicant," "What We Say," "Your Father Dead"

"Heroin" was reprinted in *The Best American Poetry 1997*.

"One Thing Certain" and "Thanksgiving" were part of a chapbook entitled *Defenestration,* which appeared in the Fall 1997 issue of *Black Warrior Review*.

ABOUT THE AUTHOR

Bob Hicok is an automotive die designer living in Ann Arbor, Michigan. He has published a chapbook, *Bearing Witness*, and *The Legend of Light*, *winner of the 1995 Felix Pollak Poetry Prize and an ALA Booklist Notable Book of the Year.*

BOA EDITIONS, LTD.: AMERICAN POETS CONTINUUM SERIES

www.ingramcontent.com/pod-product-compliance
Lightning Source LLC
Jackson TN
JSHW080854211224
75817JS00002B/28